Gho

around Bodmin Moor

Michael Williams

Bossiney Books • Launceston

Some other Bossiney books on related subjects

Dowsing in Devon and Cornwall by Alan Neal
Ghost hunting South-West by Michael Williams
Ghostly encounters South-West by Peter Underwood
Ghosts of Cornwall by Peter Underwood
Ghosts of Devon by Peter Underwood
Ghosts of north Devon by Peter Underwood
Ghosts of Somerset by Peter Underwood
Ley lines of the South-West by Alan Neal
Psychic phenomena of the West by Michael Williams
Spiritual guides in the West Country by Jane E White
Supernatural Dartmoor by Michael Williams
West country hauntings by Peter Underwood

Acknowledgements

I am indebted to those people who gave me interviews and allowed me to visit their haunted properties. As a result, we are breaking important new ground around the moor. My wife Sonia and Elaine Beckton have once more been powerful, perceptive allies. Finally thanks to Jane and Paul White for the opportunity of writing again for Bossiney.

The photographs are from the publishers' own collection.

The cover illustration shows part of the Hurlers stone circle group at Minions.

First published 2005 by Bossiney Books Ltd
Langore, Launceston, Cornwall PL15 8LD
www.bossineybooks.com
Copyright © 2005 Michael Williams
All rights reserved
ISBN 1-899383-77-8
Printed in Great Britain by R Booth Ltd, Mabe, Cornwall

The former A30 leading up to Jamaica Inn at Bolventor, a stretch of road haunted by an old green car with the roof pulled back

The ghostly character of Bodmin Moor

There is something strangely compelling about Bodmin Moor and in exploring it you may become aware of a certain strangeness within yourself. Like Dartmoor, you cannot travel many miles without encountering the mysterious – that old green car, with roof pulled back, hurtling along the A30 between Five Lanes and Bolventor; the boy in his pyjamas in the Draynes Valley; the butler who ascends the old staircase at Tredethy; the rider on horseback in the courtyard outside Jamaica Inn… the shades of this landscape are various.

There are unseen presences too: I have been on the summit of grey-green Roughtor and been aware of an invisible something or someone watching. Once I took a group of Ghost Club Society members to the Hurlers stone circles and was convinced there was more than our number present.

Some of us investigating the paranormal believe ghosts are a kind of 'tape recording', rather like the replaying of a gramophone record or a piece of old newsreel.

In a curious way Bodmin Moor challenges you not to accept everything at face value; it presents a landscape which prompts questions and analysis. Why, for example, has a small village like Altarnun so many phantoms? Are the rivers, the streams and the pools factors in the haunted reputation?

Dame Daphne du Maurier once said, while standing in a field on the edge of the moor, that she felt like 'an astronaut in time'. There is certainly a timeless quality about the place and it is quite possible that a ghost is simply a footprint in time.

Interestingly, some spirits manifest themselves very quickly after what we call death. When I first met Princess Narisa of Thailand at her old family home at Tredethy, Helland Bridge, she told me that on the night her mother passed away she was seen by people on the other side of the valley.

The nature of ghosts remains the central recurring question – and it is a difficult question because there is such diversity: ghostly people and animals, phantom trains and cars. There are even ghosts of the living and time slips. Supernatural sounds and smells, including one old house with a kitchen corridor haunted by the smell of frying onions. The list is long…

The A30 between Five Lanes and Bolventor has quite a haunted reputation, which is hardly surprising considering the thousands of people who have travelled along it, from the days of transportation by horse to the twenty-first century with its fast cars and heavy lorries.

Jacky Brown, writing from south-east London, told me: 'Some years ago we decided to drive home through the night, and beyond Jamaica Inn we were the only car on the road. Suddenly I noticed just one light following us. It appeared from nowhere and, watching it follow us in the mirror, I thought it might have been a car with a broken light. I kept thinking it would overtake us and it got very close.'

Jacky detected no outline of a car and the light vanished as quickly as it had appeared: another strand of A30 mystery.

There are various theories as to why some roads and lanes are haunted. I am sure the rerunning of old journeys – even fragments of those excursions – is a significant part of the explanation, especially if a serious accident had occurred originally. It's possible that some emotionally charged events give off a certain energy and *that* is stored in the terrain. Back in the 1920s C E Vulliamy wrote a very good book called *Unknown Cornwall*. Mr Vulliamy, who wrote equally well about crime and the landscape, had this to say about our Cornish moorland:

'Less vast, less lofty than the moors of Devon, but infinitely more mysterious, more varied in form and mood, the Cornish moors have a penetrating charm which is peculiar to themselves. In all aspects they have a strange, almost a menacing beauty; something that eludes worldly striving; mutable yet eternal, transient as the shadow of a cloud, yet steadfast as the granite of their brows…'

So, in a way, Bodmin Moor is a natural setting for manifestation.

Some of the villages have grown in the last half-century but there are other areas scarcely touched by time. Out on the grey tors a sense of mystery is increased by the loneliness of the locations, intensified when the wind whistles round the rocks.

In these wilder parts you experience an odd sense of conflict: pleasure and unease. Amid all the rugged beauty, there is a great feeling of release and renewal. You can feel curiously vulnerable because beautiful deception surrounds you. A foot in the wrong place, the ground begins to sag, oozing water – and panic is not far away. Or a thick grey mist may swiftly cover the land and you lose all sense of directions; while at night there is a strong supernatural current running across the moor.

The old folk called it Fowey Moor and, though it only stretches twelve miles north to south and eleven miles east to west, it is saturated in history and folklore. It somehow encourages ghost hunters to delve deeply. I remember having dinner with television man David Young and his wife and crew at Jamaica Inn before we did a televised interview in the haunted bedroom there. We talked about the appetite to believe in the supernatural and how this is usually matched by the compulsion to disbelieve.

There are, I suppose, people who want to be entertained or frightened by paranormal forces, but in my experience the best ghost hunts operate like well-run military exercises. Personally, I have never consciously gone researching or hunting to be 'entertained' and only twice in forty years have I been genuinely frightened.

Come then – let's see what we can discover about ghosts and supernatural activity on and around Bodmin Moor.

Spirits at the Crow's Nest

When you come to Crow's Nest, a hamlet on the eastern flank of the moor, you are in the heart of old mining country.

The Crow's Nest Inn, a lovely stonewalled building which dates

The Crow's Nest Inn, with Caradon Hill in the background

from the 1600s, is genuinely haunted. So much so, I took part in two investigations here in 2003.

Historically, there are four ghosts: footsteps heard upstairs, a lady who visits the inn for late-night drinks, a bride waiting for her lover to return from the mine, and finally an old gentleman who occasionally walks straight through the bar wall to the outside.

One man who had a crystal-clear sighting is Tony Symonds, who runs Hurlers Halt at Minions. He told me: 'It happened in 1999. I saw this woman in the style of the mid-1800s. She was medium height and had grey hair. It was about 10.30 in the evening and there were, I think, eight people present. They saw nothing, but I saw this figure in the dining room and she walked out through the window. Apparently in the past the window had been a doorway.'

A curious feature at the Crow's Nest concerns the bar clock which is always ten minutes fast. If anyone tries to correct the timing something unfortunate happens. It is as if the clock has a will of its own.

A medium, with whom I have worked for about five years, a woman of complete integrity and who prefers to remain anonymous, was with me on both investigations in 2003. On our first visit in April, using her pendulum, she quickly made contact with a spirit, but somewhat surprisingly it was not any of the 'traditional' ghosts and, through questioning, we discovered there was no link with phantom footsteps. It was actually revealed that it was the spirit of a young boy who worked in the mine and who came there to collect his wages.

In an effort to date the period in which the young man lived, we learned that he knew all about the notorious Charlotte Dymond murder on the other side of the moor in 1844. He also confirmed that the railway was running on to the moor, enabling the copper to be transported more easily. Tragically, he died early, aged only 15, in an accident down the mine. It was soon very apparent that the young miner was 'stuck' and was extremely unhappy about his inability to move on. The medium, in response, urged him to find the light and move towards it. And we believe eventually he did just that.

On our return visit in July our medium was joined by Joan Bettinson of Common Moor. Joan is one of the great characters of the moor: a 'charmer' who has become a legend in her lifetime. Apart from her considerable reputation curing animals and people, she has seen ghosts and the 'beast' of Bodmin Moor. Joan has a photographic memory and one wonders whether this might be an attribute of her charming. Though she does not claim to be a mind reader, she has the uncanny knack of reading an individual's character within minutes of meeting them.

Our medium and Joan are two very different women but, like the wise women of the old days, they are at one with Nature, their instinct and intuition finely tuned. On this second investigation a whole stream of messages came through – there were so many that we formed the impression we were in contact with more than one spirit. But the young miner, encountered earlier, had seemingly moved on.

At times the medium's pendulum whirled around violently. This was especially so when she visited the cellar and an upstairs room, which went suddenly icily cold. She was also drawn to an area which was the former staircase, now blocked in.

There were references to a local man who had gone out to New Zealand in 1877. Joan's clairvoyance established that date and the medium confirmed his death in that year. Throughout the session both psychics picked up some connection with a strange death at the inn, but in a curious way the Crow's Nest still clings to ancient secrets.

An unusual more recent event in the bar was recalled by landlord Tim Benshea. About two months previously, at around midnight, a dozen or so glasses were shattered. Tim said: 'There was no logical explanation, because the glasses were at the back of the shelf and those at the front were untouched.'

But overall the inn has a warm, friendly aura. You get the feeling that many people, through the years, have enjoyed convivial hours at the Crow's Nest. So much so that perhaps some of them are reluctant to leave it for good. In its distinctive way, this place is a vivid example of why Bodmin Moor has such a haunted reputation.

And what did Joan Bettinson make of it all?

'There is a lot of psychic activity here,' she said. 'And the stonework in and around the inn is very powerful.'

Joan's comment about the stonework is interesting because a growing number of researchers believe there is a link between ghosts and stone. It is no coincidence, then, that Bodmin Moor and Dartmoor, with so much stone across their landscapes, are heavily haunted. We agreed too that the Crow's Nest underlines another fact about the supernatural: where ghosts appear, they are likely to reappear. Tim runs the inn with his partner Abi, helped by Tim's sister Kate Wilson. Tim said that a recent visitor had seen a shadow, which defied human explanation, between the bar door and a window in the bar – and our spirit contact readily admitted he had been 'that shadow'.

There was an intriguing postscript to the Crow's Nest activity when I called on a glorious August morning in 2004 and chatted with Kate. She confirmed that Mrs Crowe, who ran the pub for a long time years ago, swore she heard phantom footsteps on the old spiral staircase.

Abi has a sister called Sophie who baby-sits for a little boy in a cottage just across the road from the Crow's Nest, and the boy is convinced he's seen a stranger, a ghost, wandering around the cottage. Moreover the boy's father has been aware of an invisible someone or something brushing past him.

Ghost of the lonely rector at Warleggan

Warleggan is a parish overshadowed by the lonely eccentric ministry of Frederick William Densham. Densham and his parishioners were at war: they boycotted his church and he barricaded his rectory grounds. He had offended them by painting the interior of the church red, yellow and blue without consulting his church council.

But there were other complaints against Densham too. He had closed the Sunday School. He had refused to hold services at convenient times. He had converted church property to his own use. He had threatened to sell the church organ, a 1914-18 war memorial… and, finally, he had erected a barbed wire fence inside the rectory grounds.

There were various bones of contention. One day his dogs escaped, running across the moor and killing sheep. He saw the solution in 600 yards of barbed wire, 8 feet high, around his property. Although it gave the impression of a prison camp, it did keep the dogs in.

Densham's manner was autocratic and his vegetarian lifestyle in the 1930s did not impress the local farming community. Roger Farnworth, who owns Densham's old residence (now The Rookery), told me: 'Densham was out in India for a time working, I think, on the family tea plantation and he came under the influence of Gandhi. That's how he became a vegetarian. He was probably closer to Gandhi and his teachings than conventional C of E.'

Densham also held strong views against generally acceptable social activities like dances and whist drives. He was a man clearly miscast for such a Cornish parish. A while back I visited Warleggan and met Cyril Keast, a former carpenter, wheelwright and coffin maker. Cyril knew the rector well and said: 'In other circumstances he would have been a very good priest. He often attended our Methodist chapel, sitting at the back taking notes during the sermon and sometimes he invited the Methodist preacher to read the lesson in his church.

'I can still see him on dark nights carrying his hurricane lantern. In a way, he was a man forty years ahead of his time… yes, he was eccentric but he was, in many ways, a good man. He took funeral services with great dignity.'

Cyril's wife, Barbara, who at 15½ was almost certainly the youngest postmistress in the kingdom, has fond memories of Mr Densham too: 'If anyone was sick, he would visit them whether they were church or chapel.' She also recalled: 'He'd come in and buy stamps and then later you'd find the money put under the mat outside the door, maybe just a few pennies.'

Densham's years at Warleggan make surely one of the saddest, most enigmatic chapters in all Cornish church history. This man, who built a children's playground with seesaws, swings, a sandpit and a pond for toy boats, must have been very lonely. No children ever actually played in it or the grounds of the rectory where he had carefully placed tables and seats equipped with writing paper in waterproof tins. No one was entertained by the magic lantern he set up in his hall and, although three spare bedrooms were furnished to accommodate visitors, they were never used.

The parish church of Warleggan

Densham's ashes may have been scattered in a Garden of Remembrance in Plymouth, but I am certain his spirit has never left Warleggan, and other people are convinced of this too. In 1999 I interviewed Michelle Haines who, at the time, had a flat in The Rookery. We talked in the grounds on a golden sunlit afternoon and she told me, 'On four occasions this year I've been aware of a dark presence, nothing menacing despite the darkness, and twice it has stroked my arm.

'Not in a threatening or sexual way. It was rather reassuring and I am certain it was the spirit of Mr Densham. I was also aware of his presence when I was picking apples in the grounds. He seems drawn to me.'

Then one day a visitor took a photograph of two people standing outside the rectory and when the photograph was printed there was a third character, a man, in the picture. The photographer was certain he had captured Densham's ghost.

Some years ago two children had a very strange experience at Warleggan Church. Their mother, Alison Weeks, remembered a cold, grey Saturday afternoon: 'I used to be on the flower rota. It was such a dismal day and the church was always so sombre I persuaded my two young daughters to come with me, telling them it wouldn't take long. They had grown a little bored inside the church and so I sent them out to sit on the stone benches in the porch until I had finished arranging the flowers.

'About five minutes later, having cleared up the leaves and put it all into a piece of newspaper, I went out to find them.

'"Mummy, Mummy, a strange man has just come in the gate and looked at us," they chorused in some agitation.

'"Well, where is he?" I asked.

'"He went up the church path and he was wearing a long black coat," one of them said.

'"And he was carrying a stick in front of him," said the other.

'I marched up the church path, dumped the leaves and the newspaper in the bin and carried on into the newer section of the graveyard. There was no man,' Alison recalled.

'"I don't know where he's gone then, because there's certainly no man and there's no way out without passing you two either," I told them and hustled them into the car where it was warmer.

'I thought no more about it until a couple of days later I mentioned it to my friend who lived in the village and she mentioned it in passing to Barbara Keast.

'The next time I saw my friend she said that Mrs Keast was sure my daughters had seen Mr Densham. She said that he wore a long black coat and carried a stick in front of him because, although he had a limp, he didn't like to be seen using a stick.'

Only on very rare occasions did anyone – usually an occasional visitor out of sheer curiosity – attend the Rector's services. On Densham's last Sunday, a *Western Morning News* staff reporter decided to be one such visitor. He later wrote: 'I sat alone at the back of the church. Unaccompanied, the Rector sang the hymns in a loud, melodious voice slightly cracked by age.

'He did not use the pulpit but conducted the service seated in a chair at the front of the altar. "I have not stood at that altar for more than ten years," he told me afterwards.

'He preached for nearly half an hour on the inconsistency of the human race.'

Frederick William Densham, at the age of 83, was found dead on the staircase of his spacious rectory in January 1953. He had collapsed while trying to reach his bedroom and he is thought to have lain there for at least 24 hours before his body was found.

Perhaps the last thoughts on Densham should come from the late Laura Farnworth, who lived at his old home. Laura concluded a profile of him with these words:

'A page of jokes and some lecture notes taken or given at Oxford in the last century were blowing around the cellar when I took over the house. A more baffling clue to the still mysterious Rector can scarcely be imagined.'

The Druid Priest

An old, strange tale concerns a Druid priest who long ago haunted the burial mound in the Manor of Rillaton. Ancient story tellers recalled how this Druid spirit approached solitary travellers on the moor at night, the most dramatic episode involving a member of the gentry who had spent a day out hunting, and had then enjoyed a meal and drinks at a neighbouring inn.

Though intoxicated, he insisted on riding home; his route took him past the mound, not far from the Cheesewring. Suddenly the huntsman was aware of an old man in a robe holding a gold cup. Reining up his horse, he studied the old man's pallid face, eyes staring strangely. The Druid spoke no words but offered the huntsman the cup.

'How have you come to possess the valuable cup?' the rider asked.

The Druid remained silent, his outstretched hands inviting the huntsman to drink. Snatching the cup from the silent stranger, the huntsman drained it, only to be surprised when lowering it that dregs remained in the bottom. The rider drank again – and yet still dregs could be seen.

'What trickery are you up to?' he demanded angrily.

Again, no reply.

The huntsman flung the dregs in the Druid's face, throwing the cup to the ground. He then rode off into the night. A few days later the bodies of the huntsman and his horse were found in a ravine.

I have not heard of any recent sightings, so this piece of ghostly history provokes two questions. Was the Druid ghost merely folklore? Or was it a case of a genuine ghost fading? There have been instances where ghosts have become fainter and fainter, finally disappearing from the earthly scene.

It is intriguing to note that when digging in the old burial mound, the Rillaton Barrow, about 170 years ago archaeologists found a skeleton and alongside it was a beaker dating from around 1500 BC.

Dozmary Pool

Pools, especially remote ones, are full of mystery and magic. They are images of the lost and the unknown – and of potential recovery. Within a paranormal context, an increasing number of people believe pools, streams and rivers somehow trigger manifestations, all of which may be a factor in explaining the moor's 'other population'.

A pool in a dream experience often refers to our emotions. How deep, clear, cloudy, beautiful or menacing was the pool? Sir John Betjeman referred to 'a brooding melancholy, especially at evening' over Dozmary. That is true, but on a sunlit day the water really sparkles and there is a spirit of refreshment in the air.

Dozmary, then, is a place for all seasons and moods – Alan Nance, a deeply respected spiritual healer and Spiritualist, told me he and friends could get in touch with 'the other side' at this special place. He believed the vibrations were so positive that communication was achieved naturally, easily.

Certainly when I brought a party of Ghost Club Society members to the rim of water our mediums made almost immediate contact with a spirit. I had explained to the members that Dozmary was thought by many researchers to be an important Arthurian location. There is a strong Cornish tradition that after the Battle of Camlann, Sir Bedivere carried the wounded, dying king away and Arthur ordered Bedivere to throw Excalibur into Dozmary Pool. But the knight was reluctant to throw away such a wondrous sword and hid it instead.

When he came back to the king, Arthur asked him, 'What did you see?' 'Nothing!' replied Bedivere. Arthur, knowing his request had not been carried out, ordered him once again to do his bidding.

For a second time, according to Tennyson, Bedivere tried to trick the king; but the third time he did as he was asked:

> So flash'd and fell the brand Excalibur:
> But ere he dipped the surface, rose an arm
> Clothed in white samite, mystic, wonderful,
> And caught him by the hilt, and brandish'd him
> Three times, and drew him under in the mere.

Sometimes a medium is able to make contact with a spirit but fails to establish his or her identity, and this was such an occasion. We recognised the spirit of a man who knew a good deal about the area.

Moreover he assured us there was a King Arthur linked to Tintagel and he saw no conflict with Arthur being in Somerset too, as the king had a roving command. He was one of the first leaders to move his troops on horseback.

As an aside, there have been reports of Arthur's ghostly figure occasionally having been seen among the dark castle ruins out at Tintagel. Some years ago I interviewed members of a psycho-expansion group (people who claimed to have lived earlier lives) and they insisted they had been genuine Arthurian characters. They firmly related Arthur to Cornwall and, of course, here on Bodmin Moor we have King Arthur's Downs.

Other Arthur strands can be seen on the western edge of Trewortha Tor where there is a large rock basin known as 'King Arthur's Bed' and, in the old days, Trethevy Quoit was known as 'Arthur's Quoit'. Can there be smoke without fire?

Getting back to our unknown spirit from long ago at Dozmary, he knew all about Doniert, one of the last kings of Cornwall who was drowned not far away in the River Fowey in the 870s. He told us the terrain was far wilder in those days, life itself more primitive, more dangerous.

The suggestion was that King Doniert had come to grief in the vicinity of Golitha Falls where the Fowey rushes down, making a wonderful crescendo. More than once near the falls I have had the feeling of an unseen personality and Peter Underwood, the Life President of the Ghost Club Society, agreed it's very likely King Doniert revisits the place where he met his death.

Reverend Sabine Baring-Gould at St Clether

The Reverend Sabine Baring-Gould, squire and parson at Lewtrenchard, was a remarkable all-rounder: archaeologist and folklorist, song collector and hymn writer, novelist and artist, biographer and conservationist. A larger than life character, he married a Yorkshire mill girl, paid for her education and turned her into a lady. He and the ever-patient Grace raised fourteen children.

Baring-Gould made many excursions across Cornwall, often covering Bodmin Moor, rebuilding holy wells, excavating ancient burial grounds and collecting material for his books.

'Brown Willy and Roughtor are fine hills,' he reflected, 'rising out of really ghastly bogs, Crowdy and Stannon and Roughtor marshes,

*St Clether
Chapel with
the Holy Well in
the background*

worse than anything of the sort on Dartmoor...'

One of his best pieces of work was restoring St Clether's holy well and chapel near Davidstow Moor. In 2003, five of us, including my medium friend and Vanda Inman who owns the glorious old building and its enclosure, went to St Clether. The medium, using her pendulum, quickly made a connection with the spirit of Baring-Gould. We felt warmly received – surprisingly so, because in his earthly life he was fairly autocratic – and formed the opinion he regards St Clether as a kind of spiritual home, enjoying the natural environment and sense of freedom.

Almost immediately he led us to the holy well, leaving us in no doubt about its healing quality. He confirmed his interest in ghosts and ghost hunting, reminding us that when you encounter a ghost the golden rule is 'Don't move and don't speak!'

He also believed King Arthur was a genuine historical figure. He knew all about the significance of ley lines and told us he had employed divining rods. We asked him about dowsers operating as psychic detectives and he agreed they had had some notable successes. In a detailed essay on the divining rod the great man had written about a dowser tracking down three French murderers, the dowsing rod enabling the detective to follow a trail for more than twenty miles, including a journey along a river by boat.

Baring-Gould was the first Robert Stephen Hawker biographer and we asked him about Hawker's controversial deathbed conversion to the Roman Catholic Church.

For once, he seemed uncertain and, on returning to my library, that evening I re-read Baring-Gould's words on the controversy. 'I cannot decide,' he wrote, 'The testimony is conflicting… he was swayed this way and that.' So there was a notable degree of consistency.

There was an intriguing postscript to our visit to the holy well and chapel. Vanda Inman, inspired by our medium's efforts, went back to the site with her own pendulum and, for the first time, she attempted to contact Baring-Gould herself. She told me: 'I felt strange hairs standing on the back of my neck and suddenly he came through.'

I owe a special personal debt to Sabine Baring-Gould because it was he who set me on the paranormal path. My wife Sonia and I were then living at Bossiney, hard by Tintagel, and I came across the following fragment.

'According to Cornish tradition,' said Baring-Gould, 'King Arthur's golden Round Table lies deep in the earth buried under this earthen mound; only on a Midsummer night does it rise, and then the flash of light from it for a moment illuminates the sky, after which the golden table sinks again. At the end of the world it will come to the surface again and be carried to heaven, and the saints will sit and eat at it, and Christ will serve them.'

So I went to Bossiney Mound on Midsummer Eve 1965. Though there was no hint of Arthur's famous table, three of us saw strange, inexplicable lights in the windows of the Methodist Chapel.

The supernatural seeds were sown.

Apports and psychometry

When items suddenly disappear and then, after a period of time, reappear in and around our cottage we jokingly refer to them as 'apports'. This is a technical term created by Tom Lethbridge, the man they called 'the Einstein of the paranormal'. He believed 'Things vanish... at other times things appear from nowhere.'

It was my old friend Alan Nance who introduced me to the subject. Alan had lost a set of keys and he hunted everywhere in his flat and shop for them in all the likely and unlikely places. Eventually he had them replaced. 'Then, one day, months later, the original keys inexplicably were back where they belonged.' Alan was convinced it was a genuine case of apporting. Moreover he had a theory that apports are frequently related to poltergeist activity: 'a spirit of mischief'.

Such thoughts came back to me very vividly one afternoon in April 2004 when a small party of us, including two mediums, visited a remote house on the edge of Bodmin Moor.

The owner set the scene. Several years ago a man, who did outside work on the property, was having his 'crib' (packed lunch) in his usual place at the foot of the stairs in an outhouse when an invisible someone tapped him three times on the shoulder. He was, in fact, the only person in the outbuilding.

'Anyway his pincers vanished from his work bench!' said our host, 'He searched everywhere for them but all in vain. Then, about a year later, the pincers in mint condition reappeared in the centre foreground of the bench.

'It was quite incredible, and there was no rational explanation for their reappearance. Nobody had borrowed them and the man concerned was completely trustworthy.'

It so happens that, apart from ghost hunting, I am especially interested in psychometry or 'object reading' – the ability to 'read' the history of an object by holding it in your hands. The importance is the link between the person owning it and the object, a ring perhaps or a watch, something personal.

On this particular visit I was allowed to handle the pincers and did so quietly, on my own, when the other Ghost Club Society members were exploring the upstairs area of the outbuilding. Vibrations came across strongly, immediately: the pincers were somehow representative of the person who had taken them. I formed the definite impression that a man, not a woman, had whisked them away.

I reported back to our principal medium a little later and she was able to confirm that the man who had taken them was, in fact, a former blacksmith, the pincers being symbolic of his old craft.

When I was researching my first supernatural book back in the 1970s I did an interview with gifted clairvoyant Betty Lukey, then living in Withiel. It was our first meeting and what Betty Lukey knew about me would not have covered one side of a postcard. Yet, through holding my watch, she not only uncovered a great deal about my past but she also made some clear predictions about the future, all of which, I think, came true in a matter of a couple of years.

The Trippet Stones

Some locations, like some poems, repay visiting more than once. The Trippet Stones is such a place. It was the writer and painter Charles Simpson who encouraged me to acquire a taste for stone circles. Charles had painted circles in Cornwall and on Dartmoor and, in a way, he became my landscape mentor.

He once said: 'We're lucky to live in an ancient land like Cornwall. In the remoter areas you feel that man is almost a newcomer.'

The Trippet Stones on Manor Common, near Bradford, are among our lesser-known stone circles, and I invariably think of Charles whenever I come here or, more particularly, of something he wrote:

'The age at which history becomes obscure is typified by the hour of twilight when… the tokens of man dead or man alive are swallowed up. As day departs, the power in the granite rouses itself to watch the approach of night.

'They wandered abroad at such an hour many strange beings whose nature none can guess: emanations, influences, memories, shaping the little destinies which they enfold…'

There is a magical quality about this small colony of stones – they form a true circle of some 33 metres in diameter – and standing inside them I am also reminded of some words by TC Lethbridge: 'Magic has an ugly name to those who have seen black magic at work among primitive people. Others think it is completely bogus and no such powers exist. But magic is simply the use of powers of the mind not yet understood by science.'

Through his researches and experiments with the pendulum, Mr Lethbridge became convinced that stone circles were some form of storage battery for this strange power.

The Trippet Stones

In June 2003 I came to the Trippet Stones with Denyse Shorrocks, the esoteric painter from Crackington Haven. It was a beautiful morning, clouds travelling across a pale blue sky, sunlight bringing out the colours of the moor, ponies and cattle grazing in the distance. It might have been a painting by Charles Simpson himself. Such stones are an essential ingredient in the magic and the mystique of the moor – there is an age-old theory that they were Cornish maidens turned to stone for dancing on a Sunday morning. The old folk were highly superstitious. They believed if your luck was bad or you were feeling out of sorts you should walk nine times around the circle in a clockwise direction. They reckoned this ritual brought better luck and provided protection against ill-wishing.

This was Denyse's first visit to the Trippet Stones and I asked about her response to them. She was thoughtful for a few moments, then said: 'There's definitely a healing presence, especially in the recumbent stones. The circle is probably about 4000 years old and you get the impression it was a gathering place for ritual, for any of the big occasions for the tribe or tribes... feasting occasions, celebrating birthdays or the seasons.

'Yes, a multi-purpose place where people met for different celebrations. It's still full of life and is more welcoming than many of the old temples and churches. The circle's a creative place.'

She believes the quartz crystal and the energy held in the stones have a healing power. Such energy is stored in many places of worship:

'You feel it in churches like Tintagel and Morwenstow,' she said. She is also sure there will soon be major advances in understanding the paranormal: 'We are, after all, in the Age of Aquarius and, like you, I feel a major breakthrough could occur here on Bodmin Moor or on Dartmoor.'

The St Michael Line

You cannot do a supernatural tour of Bodmin Moor and not make some reference to the St Michael Line. There is now a great deal of interest in ley lines among those intrigued by the paranormal.

Back in the 1960s I interviewed the author, painter and mystic Ithel Colquhoun, then living above Mousehole. It was Ithel Colquhoun who originally told me about the St Michael Line. She believed it was a line of pre-Christian force.

An alignment of ancient sites begins down in West Cornwall and ends in East Anglia. Paul Broadhurst and Hamish Miller devote a chapter to it in their thought-provoking volume *The Sun and the Serpent* (Pendragon Press, 1989). Two Bodmin Moor sites are the Hurlers Stone Circles and the Cheesewring, both close to the village of Minions. The Cheesewring is an impressive rock formation, a remarkable sculpture crafted by Nature, and some people are convinced it was once a witch's initiation rock. Furthermore, I have heard accounts of strange noises hereabouts, sounds that have no rational explanation. At night it must be an eerie place.

As for the Hurlers they are three interlocking circles and owe their name to an ancient theory that some moor men, out hurling on a Sunday, were turned into stone for their misdeeds. Hurling, truly a Celtic sport and still kept alive at St Columb Major twice every year, is thought by some of us to be a primitive ancestor of our present day game of rugby.

The turning to stone theme appears to have a Puritan genesis and interestingly Norden, writing in 1584, knew the name but did not mention the legend.

The area in and around the circles has a powerful atmosphere and many people say they 'feel better' for a visit to the stones. I have come here in all sorts of weather – it is especially magical when snow cloaks the landscape – and there is invariably something positive in the air.

My good friend Shirley Wallis, dowser, healer, astrologer and psychic, had this to say in her book *Dowsing* (Element, 1999):

The Cheesewring lies near the Hurlers, which are shown on the front cover of this book

Dowsing has revealed that primary underground water is always present at important sites such as stone circles. This water is created by mineral reactions deep in the earth, forced upward and sideways through rock fissures into what are called "blind springs" or "domes". Sometimes a breakthrough has occurred where ancient wells, springs, or waterfalls have been found. The ancient peoples who built sacred centres over primary water and aligned them with seasonally occurring astronomical features had a knowledge that respected the laws of nature and understood how to use land-energy for a productive and harmonious life. Their scientific approach is inconceivable to modern people.

In my experience the stones and area around them have an energising quality. I sometimes feel too that the stones have a strange warmth. Margo Maeckelberghe, the distinguished Cornish painter, came here with me about three years ago and she agreed: 'The stones are far warmer than you'd expect on this grey day.'

Other people have similar stories to tell: local author and Cornish Bard Joan Rendell explained to me how at the Hurlers she placed her hands on the stones 'and felt a curious tingling sensation running through my hands and fingers'.

In the autumn of 2002 I brought a party of Ghost Club Society members to the Hurlers. After some time our mediums made a link with an unknown character from long ago, but they were unable to establish any intelligent response. It were as if there was a language barrier between them and the long dead person. This is the only time I have come across such a breakdown – there are certainly occasions when no contact is made, but never before has contact been established and yet with no intelligent exchange.

The stones, of course, are about 4,000 years old and such problems may lie in that scale of time.

Charlotte Dymond

The ghost of Charlotte Dymond, like that of the Druid Priest, is probably one which has faded, although there have been various detailed sights of her in the past. In his book *Ghosts of the South West* (David & Charles, 1973), James Turner told of an angler who spent a day out on the moor and in the early evening, when returning home, was quite convinced he saw Charlotte near the stream below Roughtor where she was murdered in 1844:

'She seemed to be intent on making her way into the moor from the road. She did not speak to him when he called good night to her, but she was quite clear to him. He described her as dressed in a gown of different colours, a red cloth shawl and a silk bonnet. "I watched her," he told his host, "and she kept stopping and shading her eyes from the sun with her hand, as if looking for someone."

In all the years I have been ghost hunting I have never met anyone who has claimed to have seen her; I have only come across a second-hand account of her being observed in Davidstow churchyard where her body was buried. I mentioned these facts to Harry Cleverly, a medium who lived at Altarnun, and he said, 'I'm not surprised Charlotte has not been seen in recent years, because I understand a service of exorcism took place near her memorial by the stream and that means she's probably gone on…'

Through psychic research and, after watching the re-enactment of Matthew Weeks's trial at Bodmin's Shire Hall, I am certain the hanging of Matthew Weeks was an injustice. Charlotte's real murderer was a jealous rival.

There are some very old accounts of Charlotte's ghost haunting the summit of Roughtor. I've been to the summit myself a score or more times and, in the days when we owned dogs, Rex, our beautiful, sensitive collie, invariably had an air of anticipation, even excitement, on the top of this glorious tor.

Rex reacted in precisely the same way on Hound Tor on Dartmoor. I told James Turner about his behaviour and he said, 'Roughtor is alive with spirits... I don't say you'll see ghosts but there are spirits up there.'

Some of us strongly suspected that James was in love with Charlotte Dymond. He would not be the first or last man to fall for an attractive female ghost. In his excellent collection of short stories entitled *Staircase to the Sea*, his thirteenth story, 'Love Affair', opens with these words:

"'Charlotte,' I begged, "you can't leave me forever, you can't." I hardly knew, in my grief, what I was saying or the appalling implications of my words. I knew only that that was what she intended, that she could not help herself, and that nothing I could do would be of the slightest use, "It's unfair to leave me after what we have shared. Don't you know the meaning of love?"'

I never come to Charlotte's memorial stone on the edge of the moor, with awe-inspiring views of Roughtor, without thinking of them both. James's ashes were scattered here.

Not many people know that Aleister Crowley, the *bête noir* of the paranormal, visited Roughtor – some even hint he held a black mass on the summit one night. I remember a conversation with Peggy Garside, a neighbour in our Bossiney years. Peggy, a worldly woman who had nothing to do with black magic, had met Crowley socially and she found him 'a delightful man'. But she was flabbergasted to learn that she 'had drunk cocktails and had danced on a ballroom floor with the most wicked man in the world!'

Jamaica Inn

Jamaica Inn, immortalised by Daphne du Maurier's novel of the same name, is the most haunted inn in Britain. In *Ghost Hunting South-West* (Bossiney, 2003) I wrote at some length about strange goings-on here, and now I will add more data to the continuing paranormal saga.

In October 1998 I was a member of the Ghost Club Society team

Jamaica Inn

which investigated Jamaica Inn. That night, between the hours of 11 pm and 2 am there was almost a kind of psychic electricity in the atmosphere. We had a remarkable sighting.

The small bar, where nine of us were present, was dark but some light was reflected from the main bar. Five of us saw a man sitting in a chair or it might have been on a bench. Two were unsure about the sighting and the last two did not see anything. When the lights went back on, the man had disappeared and, significantly, I noticed that a collection of logs in a container stood before the area where the man had been seen. At the time of the sighting I was not aware of these logs and, when the lights revealed the present day geography of the room, there was no sign of a chair or bench. We had quite simply experienced a time slip – and had viewed that part of the room as it had once been years ago.

The man had not belonged to modern times. He was dark but not all that distinct – like a painting that has faded somewhat through age. He was there – I have no doubt about that – and he somehow generated the impression of a person on business.

Jamaica at night assumes a different character. When the customers have left the bars, and the residents have gone to bed, it is as if the inn slips back in time and there is an air of expectation about the place. On this night I felt we were truly at the edge of the unknown.

On a more recent Ghost Club Society visit in April 2001, the small bar produced another intriguing experience. It was again what I would call full of atmosphere when I and others in the party smelt tobacco. It was a strong whiff of pipe tobacco, nothing at all like a modern cigarette. Curiously, that smell went and later came back – as if confirming that supernatural forces were at work.

The really impressive fact about Jamaica Inn is that in the more than four decades I have known the place, a steady stream of staff and visitors have given first-hand accounts of events which defy logical explanation. There have been so many that I am convinced the inn boasts not one ghost but several.

I have taken part in two television programmes at the inn and nothing of a paranormal nature occurred on either, but in 2004 ghost hunters in Living TV's *Most Haunted* series said they were terrified by a night spent there. They claimed to have had a dramatic experience in bedroom 5 and in an outbuilding housing an electricity generator.

Presenter Yvette Fielding seemed visibly shaken as she explained to viewers that she saw a reflection of a woman, wearing a bonnet-type hat, in the bottom corner of an ornate mirror of bedroom 5.

As for the generator room, there were claims that objects were thrown at the team and Miss Fielding, looking towards the roof said, 'I can see shapes… the outline of a figure.'

Shortly after that programme was transmitted, journalist Ben Glass of *The Cornish Guardian* spent a night in the haunted bedroom and he later wrote:

'The only incident that was mildly strange was waking in the middle of the night and finding I was unable to move. Lying on my side I awoke with the sense that someone was near the cupboard behind me but despite efforts I could not summon the strength to actually turn and look and fell back into slumber.

'However, since I've had this paralysis-type experience before I wouldn't judge this event to be particularly ghostly. My imagination was probably getting the best of me.'

Nevertheless Martin Watts, the general manager of the inn, told Ben that many guests occupying bedroom 5 had been woken during the night to find a woman dressed in eighteenth-century clothing looking over them. Mr Watts further explained that a former innkeeper – date unknown – had murdered a woman because she was the mother of his illegitimate child. He said other ghosts upstairs included an American airman whose body was brought to the inn after he had crashed on the moor. He added that numerous guests had been so frightened by a sighting they had absconded during the night. 'Only the other week, one lady got the manager up saying she wanted to leave. But he managed to calm her down and she stayed.'

The impressive feature of Jamaica's reputation is that it's an ongoing story. Only recently I was talking to Dawn Hooper, as she was when I first knew her, a teenager working at the inn. Dawn recalled: 'Working there back in the 1950s I had live-in accommodation and I remember my bedroom overlooked the courtyard. Every morning, without fail, the door of my wardrobe would be open. I never saw anything but that wardrobe door; something or someone opened it every night… even though my bedroom door was locked.'

Reginald Carthew, the bearded barman at Jamaica, once said, 'Many times I felt I was being watched. I'd turn round and there would be nobody there.'

More than a dozen people over the years have spoken to me about hearing invisible footsteps pacing the upstairs corridor and, on checking, finding it deserted.

Individually, these may seem rather matter-of-fact happenings but collectively they underline the continuing paranormal activity. Add to them the sightings reported in *Ghost Hunting South-West* and you understand why Jamaica is like a solid granite tor of the paranormal.

A frightening experience in Bodmin

One of my most frightening experiences in forty years of ghost hunting took place at the former Maple Leaf Café in Bodmin, now renamed the Providence Café.

To begin at the beginning: it was in September 2001 when seven members of the Ghost Club Society and chief reporter Ian Shepherd of *The Cornish Guardian* visited the café. I had no doubt the shop was haunted: an earlier reconnaissance with a medium and a conversation with people connected with the café all clearly indicated that 'someone' occasionally called, usually around 4 o'clock in the afternoon. So naturally we assembled at 3.30.

Opposite: The Providence Café and Financial Advice Centre, Bodmin

Sometimes seen but more frequently heard, 'he' had the habit of climbing the narrow staircase, still hoping to find his long lost lover. Our medium uncovered a good deal of information about this man – he had been a soldier with the Duke of Cornwall Light Infantry during the 1914-18 war, and his complicated love life involved his sister-in-law. It was another case of unknown identity.

Perhaps at this point I should explain how the medium operates. She has a piece of rock crystal which is attached to a string, forming a pendant. There is a long paranormal tradition that the pendant swings in different directions, answering 'Yes' or 'No' when specific questions are put to a co-operative spirit. There are occasions when sometimes the spirit will respond only grudgingly – and infrequently they even decline to make any response at all.

On this Saturday afternoon the spirit of the old soldier was responding well until Trevor Kenward, a very experienced investigator and a senior officer in the Ghost Club Society, asked a question which clearly touched a raw nerve.

Ian Shepherd, in *The Cornish Guardian* on the following Thursday, wrote: 'But when Trevor posed the question: "Did your sister-in-law go off with another man?," the pendant sharply indicated "Yes" and then gyrated at high speed, with the medium struggling to hold on until the device broke, releasing the crystal, like a sling-shot, into Mr Kenward's face.'

The crystal did, in fact, damage Trevor's lower lip, splitting it open and causing a second wound inside the lower lip, a flow of blood lasting about twenty minutes. In the words of the medium, 'I could feel real anger. It was frightening and I've never experienced anything like it.'

While Trevor tended his wounds, a new pendant was shaped using the same crystal and a new piece of twine. When questioning resumed, the medium asked the spirit, 'Was it an accident?' The pendant whizzed at increasing speeds before again flying off in the direction of Trevor Kenward, but luckily missing him.

Later Trevor concluded the study by holding the pendant in his left hand, saying: 'The spirit which was contacted through the medium is now demanded in the name of the Father, the Son and the Holy Ghost to depart in peace.'

Gradually we felt a transformation in the atmosphere and peace returned to the room. The then proprietor of the Maple Leaf, Fiona Thompson, told me in two subsequent conversations that they had not seen or heard anything unusual since our Saturday afternoon visit. She was sure the troubled spirit had moved on.

Oddly enough though, there was a follow-up of these incidents in that in August 2004 Andrew Harvey of the Financial Advice Centre, next door to the café in Honey Street, reported strange happenings in his offices – a main door opening and closing several times for no apparent reason, lights going on and off, and the mechanism of a safe jamming mysteriously... and all this happening within a few weeks of the office opening. Andrew's wife Patricia probably summed it up when she said, 'There's something not quite right about the place...'

Anyway, our medium made a visit and we were both immediately aware of the very oppressive atmosphere in the back office. The medium made a connection with the spirit of a young man called Albert who died in mysterious circumstances in the 1800s and who indicated he died next door in what is now the café. Was it murder? Or was it suicide?

The office and the café may well be worth further investigation. There is no doubt that Honey Street, Bodmin, is full of paranormal possibility – perhaps it's on a ley line.

Some final reflections

Time remains the huge enigma. Not for nothing did Professor Joad refer to 'the undoubted queerness of time...' I believe that when someone sees a ghost, he or she is looking out from their time frame and observing events in another.

Touring haunted Bodmin Moor has been a revealing experience, an opportunity for assessment and reassessment, the excursions roughly coinciding with revisiting J B Priestley's book *Man & Time*. In it Mr Priestley offers the interesting theory that there are three 'mes'. The first 'me' is when I observe passively, almost as if half asleep. The second 'me' is when I'm fully awake and aware, focusing my attention. The third 'me' emerges when engaged in purposeful activity – and am unable to observe in a detached way. Bodmin Moor somehow proves the quality of such reasoning.

Today a growing body of evidence is building up in support of the supernatural, including written statements, often collaborated by a second or third person, and strange sights on film – like the ghostly figure captured on camera at Hampton Court in 2003. I wrote to *The Times* of London on the subject and this is the letter they published:

Phantoms on film
From Michael Williams

Sir, The ghostly figure caught on film at Hampton Court (report and photograph, December 20) may well be genuine. As a ghost hunter for more than 40 years, I hope so. Evidence for the existence of ghosts is building up.

My library contains dozens of photographs, many in published books, all defying human explanation. The next 50 years will surely produce more ghosts on films and sounds on tape.

The cynics are on shaky grounds.

Yours faithfully
Michael Williams
(Council member Ghost Club Society)
Cornwall

Last year scientists found evidence that human beings may indeed possess a 'sixth sense'. John Elliott and Sarah Keenlyside, writing in *The Sunday Times* on 27 June 2004, said: 'researchers at Freiburg University, one of Germany's oldest and most respected academic institutions, have been surprised by the experiments which suggest humans could have paranormal powers.

'They conclude that the eerie sensation of being watched by an unseen observer – the staple of many a horror film – may not be just a figment of the imagination.'

On a golden June afternoon in 2004 I called on Joan Bettinson, a true 'wise woman', at her home near Minions. I asked her why Bodmin Moor is steeped in hauntings and mysteries.

She was silent for a few moments.

'Well,' she said, 'it's a bit like Dartmoor, another haunted moor. So many dramatic events have happened and there's a strong sense of the past out on the moor, as if you're going back into the mists of time.

'Tragedies down the mines, things like that have left their mark. A lot of water too – ghosts often show up near water.'

Colin Wilson in his *Directory of Possibilities* (Webb & Bower, 1981) has said of auras: 'Living creatures are surrounded by an electrical energy field… the ancient Egyptians sometimes show halos around the heads of the gods or important people… for many centuries, occultists and mystics have described a halo surrounding the whole human body.'

Trethevy Quoit, once called Arthur's Quoit. This stone tomb, originally covered with a barrow, served an ancient village near St Cleer some 5000 years ago. Such ancient sites on the Moor provoke a strong sense of the past

Joan agreed and went on to say, 'In the days when I delivered post in the Fowey Valley I often picked up auras and one day cycling down it I felt an aura around me... like a strange cloak closing all around me.'

Joan's first ghostly encounter was when she was in her twenties: 'I was doing some cooking in the kitchen of our home at Commonmoor, formerly known as Catts Chapel, named after the minister who was defrocked for getting a young girl pregnant.

'I was taking some cakes out of the oven when this apparition appeared: a young girl in a straw hat with buttercups. I guessed she was the unfortunate girl he'd made pregnant. She was very pretty.

'Various members of the family swore they saw a preacher chap, dressed in black in the house. We assumed it was the Reverend Catts coming back.

'I believe that when you have tragedies, especially events involving the emotions, then they're likely to trigger spirits. Some things just come back.'

Joan's son Charles, a keen angler, also told me an eerie tale: 'I was riding close to a derelict farm called Little Siblyback below Kilmar Tor, with my dogs running loose. Suddenly there was this incredible sound like dozens of chandeliers tinkling… like stereo sounds. The animals freaked out. The three dogs shot off and the horse bolted. These strange sounds stopped just as suddenly as they started. I explored the old farmhouse on foot, or what was left standing… and there was not a soul about… all very weird.'

Bodmin Moor, then, has this ongoing haunted reputation. It also reminds us that we live in times of exciting change and challenge. Paranormal evidence is becoming stronger and stronger, more and more responsible people are searching and researching – major break-throughs are surely ahead.

One day or one night, maybe sooner than you might expect, possi-bilities and probabilities will become realities.

Will Bodmin Moor feature in these unfolding events?

I like to think it truly will.

A naturally occurring logan stone near Roughtor. The granite has its own mysteries